First Kiss

Encompassing Techniques For Initiating The Initial Kiss, Ensuring Minimal Resistance From The Partner, And Potentially Eliciting A Desire For Further Intimacy

Francis Archer

Gavin awoke moments before the sun rose above the hills encircling his family's ranch. When he returned from his trip to Dallas to buy hay, he hadn't closed the blinds yet, or perhaps he had done so this morning. Attempting to shade his face from the sun, he raised an arm and placed it across it. He felt his body ache as he turned over, and his brain throbbed as he struggled to recall why.

"Awful!" He squinted at the clock, opening one eye. A little after six a.m. He should have gotten up and rode to the back pasture when he stopped at Kayla's for breakfast. Mike informed him yesterday night, or possibly the night before, that an additional five or six heads of cattle had gone missing.

Already, their numbers had dropped to under a thousand. The ranch was in danger of failing; more losses were beyond their means.

He let his feet drop to the floor as he swung his long legs over the side of the bed. He sat there with the palms of his callused hands pushed against his eyes for a few minutes. The room's lighting was nearly intolerable. When he finally raised himself to his feet, he winced as he extended his strong arms above his head. His right shoulder was hurting. On unsteady legs, he grimaced and walked over to the dresser. The events of last night came back to me when I saw his face in the mirror.

He recalled taking his hay guy, Matt, to a bar. He knew a lot of whiskey—Jim

Beam, specifically—involved. He believed that a girl might have been present—yes, a girl was present. She was the bartender with the body of a goddess, the face of an angel, and a lover who looked like King Kong. Her failure to bring up the boyfriend had been the issue. She did not give Gavin a kiss in the alley as she would have if they were a boyfriend, and she headed outside for her break. The biggest fist he had ever seen concluded, which was his first indication that she had any commitments. In less than a second, the female Candy began telling King Kong that Gavin had approached her and wouldn't accept no. He had been lying on the pavement on the butt of his Wranglers. Although Gavin was a large man, King Kong was far larger. If he hadn't been drinking, he might have known better than to say anything. But sadly, he wasn't.

He recalled saying something like, "She never said no," as he looked at the enormous man.

Looking back, it was clear it had been the incorrect thing to say. The large, hairy ape, who appeared to have become disoriented in the evolutionary process, reached down, lifted him, and knocked him down again. By then, Gavin was too drunk and more than a little irritated to grasp that King Kong may become bored and move on if he stayed down. There was a fight, if you could even call it that, and when King Kong eventually got tired of it, he took his girl and ran away.

With his black, curly hair sticking up in eighteen different places and his already weathered and sun-bronzed skin covered in thick stubble, Gavin stood in front of the mirror and pondered when his life would ever stop being a string of drunk one-night affairs. Or, like what happened to him last night—a vicious beating over a lady he would have only ever had one sexual encounter with. Perhaps after sorting out the mess, the ranch was in, perhaps then. Or perhaps it was when he could go past that threshold and truly trust a lady. He was a woman's man. He was enamored with both their fragrance and taste. He liked touching and observing them. He was going to need them, no question about it. Though he had the same desires as any other man, despite being young and in good health, he could not trust them enough to go farther. Although he hadn't always been this way, that was the past; this was, and probably always would be his present.

He threw on a t-shirt to cover up his bulky build, picked up his jeans from the ground, and tucked them in. He felt concerned about explaining the split lip and black eye to his sister while cleaning his face. He could already see her pouting, shaking her head, and yelling, "Gavin, when will you ever grow up?"

Kayla was one of those persons who was born thirty-five, and it wasn't his fault. She planned everything out and gave careful attention to every action. She was anything but impulsive, which was why Kayla was the one really in charge of the ranch, while Gavin had spent his entire life getting into problems.

He jolted out of his trance when there was an unbearably loud knock on his front door, and he started beating his head again.

"Hi, Gavin! Are you joining me on our ride to the back-passure? I would hate to skip breakfast. You are aware of how your sister is.

With half-open eyelids, Gavin pulled open the door and glanced at Mike. The ranch worker laughed when he spotted his employer. "What girl did you make out with last night?"

Why do you suppose it has to do with a woman? Gavin questioned, glancing away from the door to get his boots.

Mike entered after him. It always seems to be about a lady with you, boss. When did your sister last see you?

Gavin remained silent. He pulled on his long-sleeved shirt and put on his boots. "Lead the way."

As he left, he slapped himself and took his dusty brown Stetson off the hook near the door. He was relieved to discover that Satan, his favorite black stallion, was waiting for him and that Mike had already saddled the horses. He grunted loudly, slung his still unsteady leg over the saddle, and stepped into the stirrup. Mike gave up, attempting to contain his laughter.

"Cease talking!" Gavin informed him before sneering at Satan. A Queensland called Bo and a Catahoula Leopard named Sue trailed behind him as he and Mike rode out of the yard. The slender little goat that trailed behind them was the only peculiar thing about it. Clarence was a goat that was abandoned, and Bo and Sue had decided to take care of him. That was good, but Gavin lacked the courage to tell Clarence the truth, so now he felt like a dog.

It was a gorgeous early September morning in Texas. It was blowing a cool breeze. They had not felt a breeze since late spring. Perhaps summer was finally ending, and the seasons were shifting.

Gavin inhaled the clean, pleasant air. The smell of the countryside and the feel of the warm sun on his face were the two things he loved the most in the world.

Only three hundred yards separated them from his cabin when Mike yelled, "What the—what in the world?"

Gavin could instantly smell the smoke, so he didn't even need to inquire what he was talking about. He glanced in the direction Mike was staring at, up to the large ridge behind the rear field and, with the proper wind, directly into the main house and stables. After observing the flames scorching the parched, amber-colored hill for a short while, he turned to Mike and hurriedly said, "I'll grab the truck." Grab Clint, grab a few shovels, and ride quickly. I'm going to hurry over and get Kayla. It appears to be aiming toward the main home.

"You've got it, boss."

Gavin pressed the heel of his boot against Satan's side. All the horse needed to know was that he meant business. As they returned to the cottage, Gavin slid off and dashed for his keys. Satan had already returned to the barn when he emerged to his truck. After grinning at that, he went to get his sister and took out his phone.

***

Kayla heard the pickup approaching on the dirt road while brewing coffee in the kitchen. She reached for her hat and boots. She was certain Gavin would never speed up that road unless it meant the difference between life and death. She was on the porch when he stopped before the home and applied the brakes.

"Do I have to finish it right here?"

Jenna Jameson is the most popular girl in my class and owns it. The entire area is currently decked out like a Christmas tree.

Why? since Jenna turns eighteen today. Naturally, her home is prepared for a lavish celebration. I suppose nothing but the best for the only child of two successful lawyers.

I and the whole Colson High senior class are invited despite her hatred of me.

It's alright. It's a reciprocal feeling.

Which is precisely the reason I initially refused to attend. Why would I voluntarily enter a hostile situation, then? But Lewis and Becca, my closest pals, made me.

All as a result of one foolish dare. Specifically, a kissing dare.

The kissing challenge that I foolishly accepted. However, I never back down from a challenge. Regardless of the difficulty, I consistently persevere.

However, regarding this one? Better spoken than done.

Nell, please be serious. You've taken many risks. Becca informs me from the front passenger seat, "This should be a piece of cake to you," while she puts on lip gloss and doesn't take her eyes off the sun visor reflection.

I give her a back-of-the-head grimace. "This one is different, you know that."

"Because he used to be Jenna's boyfriend?" Lewis, who is supposed to drive tonight, smirks at me as he twists in the driver's seat.

"Or because it'll be your first kiss?" Becca finally says, peering over her shoulder with her all-too-perceptive glare.

Oh no. I sometimes detest how well they know me.

As they are not incorrect. These are the main two factors that make this a terrible idea. Still, why did they have to challenge me to a kiss with Caleb Castillo? Really, of all the boys and all the dares?

I give them both a fierce look. "What about the two?"

Becca chuckles. "Oh, please, hurry up. It will be enjoyable. Imagine that your first kiss won't be monotonous. It will be the kind of first kiss you can proudly tell others about.

I wrinkle my nose. And for heaven's sake, why would I tell anyone about my first kiss?

Becca shrugs. "Yes, I did."

Lewis responds, "Same."

"Well, I'd rather not talk about it."

Becca gives an eye roll. Alright. Kiss the boy and keep it private.

"It goes without saying, but not from us," Lewis quickly adds, winking.

I give him the finger of accusation. "However, you're not posting it on TikTok."

We have a shared TikTok account where we share our completed dares. Over the years, it has accumulated half a million followers, making us a celebrity at school, which my pals eat up wholeheartedly.

We started the dares our freshmen year simply out of boredom one day. And the regulations are not too complicated. Whoever draws the two longest straws gets to challenge the person who draws the shortest. We draw straws. We each get three consecutive dares since the loser cannot be dared twice.

Dangerous dares are forbidden. At least it's not too risky.

I've cherished the game forever.

That is until they gave me the challenge this afternoon.

It seems unlikely that they made it up at the moment, as is typically the case. The cunning little brats have this all figured out. Perhaps all they want is an excuse to attend the party or something similar.

Either that, or they decided it would be wise to give me my first kiss before my eighteenth birthday. Which is coming up in three months.

Whatever. This still bothers me.

They simply wait for their short sticks to arrive. Nothing stoops to the level of a loser scorned.

Lewis gives me a grin full of teeth. "I will attempt."

My eyes enlarge. "Lewis Jon Jones, you need to put in more effort!"

He flinches. "You have to put my middle name in there?"

Now it's my turn to smile toothily. "Always."

Alright, Nelly. Are you prepared? Becca queries.

"Not just yet." I go inside my clutch purse for my tiny mirror, checking whether I need to touch up my makeup. Luckily, though, I don't. Even with no makeup, I still look great. However, my long, chocolate-brown hair... "Yes, give me a minute."

****

I tell Becca, "I'm still not happy that I'm doing this," as I clink my red cup.

As anticipated, nearly too many people are attending the party at Jenna's house. Instead, we have decided to hang out by the pool. Even though there are many people here, there are seats available. The music is still audible to us—just not as loudly.

Jenna and I haven't met yet, which is fantastic since I'll have to wish her a happy birthday.

That will be awful, not even that I want her to know I'm here.

Before responding to me, Becca waved at the person who had just waved at us. "Well, as you always say, a dare is a dare and needs to be done."

"Aww. Please don't hold my words against me.

"Why not? You constantly turn people against us.

It is accurate. Whenever they whine about their assignments, I always remind them of that. I even refer to them as "chicken" at times. Yes, I'm not exactly the most polite person when I play the game.

And now it's the other way around.

I'm not comfortable here.

"What is the experience like when you taste your own medicine?" Lewis laughs over to my right.

I give him a tongue-out.

He merely chuckles.

Becca responds, "I think you should find Caleb right now."

We recently arrived here. May I go finish my drink before you do?

"This is rosy lemonade. It can be completed in one sitting.

"Well, I'm just taking in the scenery right now."

They both tilt their fair hair towards me and ask, "What view?" together.

I think they are twins when they act like that for a split second. They're not. The real twins are their mothers. Because of this, they appear to be exact replicas of one another, which usually makes me happy and annoys them. People also assume that they are twins.

I gesture across the pool to the couple indulging in each other's faces. "It's sentimental."

Becca sneers. It's not sentimental. It's repulsive.

It is accurate. We've been in this location since the makeout session began. At this point, it's become an eyesore.

Well, anything. It beats me doing my dare to watch them. At least I can delay the inevitable.

"Oh, without a doubt." Lewis then exclaims, "Hey, horndogs! Take a room.

"Lew, tell 'em," Becca chuckles.

The pair gives us a sneer before getting up and walking away from their private moment.

Fantastic. That ends my justification.

Lewis and Becca wag their heads at me as if they can read my thoughts.

I scoff. "I'm working on it. Geez.

The initial kiss.

Kelly is helped out of bed by the yells from below and the sunlight peeking through the curtains. She realizes instantly that the momentous day has finally arrived. She jumps out of bed, runs fearlessly down the stairs, grabs a quick drink, hurries back upstairs, and carefully completes her daily ritual before heading to school.

Kelly doesn't even hear her mother's call before running out of the house, leaving her brother and sister behind. She is racing to school, giggling, skipping, and being very enthusiastic. Kelly's lunch date today is with Luke, a charming and witty young man who attends her class. She exhaled deeply as she entered the first session and realized he wasn't there. She had forgotten that they weren't in the same class, so time felt slower.

After the first session, Luke is in the math class, his short hair in a stylish mess. He's dressed in blue Adidas tracksuit pants and a white t-shirt with the Nike tick emblem. When Kelly sees him in the distance, her heart skips a beat. He glances up and gives her a modest smile, which she responds with an equally sly smile.

She tried to focus throughout the lesson, but her thoughts were racing. Her young pals grew increasingly irritated with her since they could never persuade her to help them with math. She was so focused on making lunch go smoothly that it consumed her thoughts.

Luke once tried to talk to her, but she shook her head. He was disappointed, but this wasn't the place to talk; too many little ears were waiting.

It was break time, and she had gone out laughing and chatting with her pals. She thought everything was dull as they talked about the typical things—boys, clothes, and professors. She joined in with a semblance of sincerity but watched Luke play football with his mates.

Next is a history lesson, with the teacher reading aloud from a book. The history of the Tudors and Stuarts is so dull that Kelly could not concentrate. Mrs. Lilley, her instructor, had finally had enough of her refusal to pay attention and to respond to questions.

After dismissing her from the classroom, she sent her to her spouse, the headmaster.

She was summoned directly to his office and required to explain her actions of disobedience. Since Kelly is often a great student, he is soothing and cool, so he lets her off with a warning and some advice to get herself in order. She is then instructed not to visit his office again should it escalate.

When the bell rings, and it's time for lunch, Mr. Lilley gently encourages her to go and sends her on her way with a kind grin. She can't stop the butterflies from entering her stomach at this point. At the hall's entry, Kelly spots Luke. He gives a modest smile but stays silent. She can hardly taste any of their lunches as they eat them together at the table in near silence.

After they finished their lunches, the hall appeared cramped, with an excessive number of small eyes and ears. They were not seated with their normal companions and had already drawn attention from others in the hallway. Kelly put her hand in Luke's after they were outdoors, and he gave her his first genuine smile, giving her the confidence she had been missing.

In contrast to the stuffy hall, the air here is pure and fresh, and the sun makes the day warm. Talking and laughing, Kelly tells him she has been expelled from the class but withholds the whole reason. She claimed it was because of too much talking and that she didn't want Luke to get arrogant and tell his buddies how much of an impact he made on her.

After lunch, the bell sounds again, bringing a foreboding sound. Reluctantly and hesitantly, they stand up. Anxious that this is their first meeting, the young couple laughs and lunges at each other, clashing noses uncomfortably. Then, they tentatively kiss. Kelly steps aside. Luke reaches out to kiss her again, but she says no, kisses his nose instead, and runs off laughing.

Kelly turns to face Luke, resting on his back and gazing at the sky. She knows he feels the same way she does. She gives a huge sigh and a big smile. The world has greatly improved since then!

Historical Letters

The date on the postmark is May 14, 1944. Oh my, Grammy would have only been eighteen then, almost nineteen. Even though I'm a little awkward about prying into Grammy's private life, I remove the delicate paper from the envelope.

You probably never imagined that I would write, yet here I am, my lovely English Rose, and all because I just can't seem to get you out of my brain.

Who would have guessed? After spending a night dancing with you at the USO club, I can't stop thinking about you. On Saturday, I had no intention of going at all. I missed my family in the United States and didn't want to be in England.

Life is weird that way. I would never have met my English Rose with the golden hair and brilliant blue eyes if my mates hadn't demanded that I accompany them instead of languishing in self-pity.

As soon as I stepped in, you caught my attention. You were laughing and enjoying yourself while seated with several pals. You invited us to sit at your table, and it seemed petty to hold onto my sorrows amid such cheerful companionship.

Even though I don't usually dance, I had to beg for some alone time with you. I'm not skilled enough to be considered a dancer, but while you were in my arms, I felt like I was floating. You never stopped laughing or smiling, and the twinkle in your baby blues illuminated the room, even when I stepped on your toes. I believe I may have developed a slight romantic interest in you at that time.

Those few dances banished my blues. Now that I'm back at camp, I can only think about you.

I will understand if you don't reply, but I hope you do.

Marlon

Whoa, Grammy had a wartime admirer. My gaze dropped to the picture. Is that dude Marlon? I'm eager to learn more. I reach quickly for the next letter, dated June 22, 1944.

I, a poor guy from Brooklyn and the son of a shopkeeper, hoped and never thought you would write back, my lovely

English Rose. I worry that responding to your queries will take up this entire letter.

Your initial inquiry concerned my origins, to which I have previously responded, but allow me to elaborate: Brooklyn is a city in New York. Indeed, I sincerely wish to return there in the future—as much as I can in this insane world.

Despite being in the Air Force, I'm not a pilot—that's very different. Therefore, I cannot declare myself among the heroes who supported the D-Day landings by air.

As a mechanic, I dedicate all my time to maintaining those aircraft in the air. Last year, I wanted to enroll in college to study electrical engineering, but as it is,

I'm employed in a different capacity. No, I don't want to think that way in case I jinx things, perhaps when the war is finished.

Hearing about your family was fascinating. Isn't it ironic that your father, like mine, is a retailer? I was sorry to learn that your mother passed away when you were little. Your older sister must have found it difficult to take on her role.

Although she is younger than I am and is still in high school, I also have a sister. Although my mother wants her to become a nurse, she is more interested in joining the military after graduation. The next time I write, I'll inform her about your job as a chauffeur for the upper echelons of the brass; I do not doubt that she would prefer to work in a similar capacity.

I'll be able to visit London again at the end of July. I'll watch for you at the USO if I don't hear from you before then.

With the utmost respect,

Marlon

My mind is racing. Grammy corresponded with Marlon, attempting to get to know him rather than just being an admirer. The mail I take up after that is smaller and without a postmark.

Having to go through censors and all, I wasn't sure if my reply would reach you in time when I received your letter, my lovely English rose. I'm asking a friend from home for a favor. He says he will drop it off at your headquarters. He drives for the big shots in the Air Force.

I will recognize you if we cross paths at the station since I will always connect deeply with you. I have scheduled my leave for the final weekend of July. On Friday, we arrive by train at approximately 4 p.m. I could take you out to supper, maybe.

I'll head to the USO, where we met on Saturday night, just in case we don't see each other at the station.

I'm keeping track of the minutes until our next meeting.

Marlon

Did they get together? The letter that follows is dated August 5, 1944. I'm trying everything not to rip it out of its envelope.

My sweet English Rose,

My heart pounded when I saw you waiting on the platform, still wearing your uniform and stretching your neck to find me. I'm glad I'm tall because I soon found you practically lost in the crowd, but my gaze never strayed from you, and before long, we were together.

I had to tell myself that we had only recently met, yet even though I felt like I knew you so well, I still wanted to embrace and kiss you.

I was content with how your face brightened when I showed up, and my pulse raced as you put your arm through mine, leaned in, and said, "Hello, airman," in your gorgeous accent. How about taking a female out to dinner?

I would have been content to stare at you across the table. I wasn't sure whether we would talk much during our lunch. We didn't stop talking to give the waiter our order, and for me to pay the bill, so I didn't need to worry.

How I wished the night would never end. Reluctant to let you go, I accompanied you to the underground since you had to go home before curfew. I got you to commit to meeting the next day so you could show me around London before you departed.

My Rose, those views were nothing compared to you. Even if there had not been a battle, you would have exceeded all I saw that day, despite what you may have told me.

Being apart from my family is now more than manageable thanks to the two days I spent with you, Rose, and I feel fortunate to have met you. I'm hoping you share my sentiments.

Until our next meeting, Marlon

Oh my god, throughout the war, Grammy was in love with someone else. It was like reading a love story when you read the notes Marlon wrote her. Why hadn't Grammy said anything? Was it that Grandpa never found out?

Pick up a new skill: Decide which skill you've always wanted to learn, then put in the time and effort to get it. Learning new talents, whether in cooking, public speaking, coding, or playing an instrument, can increase your self-assurance and open up new opportunities.

Engage in introspection: Make time every day for introspection. You can develop personal growth and self-awareness through journaling, meditation, or silent reflection to better understand who you are, what you stand for, and what your objectives are.

Develop an optimistic outlook: Positive affirmations should be used to counter negative ideas. Embrace gratitude, live in the present, and surround yourself with supportive people to cultivate an upbeat and hopeful outlook.

Develop wholesome relationships by surrounding oneself with uplifting, encouraging, and helpful people. Make an effort to keep lines of communication open and honest while fostering your relationships.

Accept failure as a teaching opportunity: See failure as a springboard for development and education rather than something to be afraid of. Accept responsibility for your mistakes, grow from them, and utilize them as motivation to become a better person.

Establish measurable objectives consistent with your values and aspirations to create meaningful goals. Divide them into more manageable goals and make concrete plans to achieve them.

Establish boundaries, prioritize self-care, and schedule time for hobbies, leisure, and spending quality time with loved ones to cultivate a healthy work-life balance. Maintaining a healthy work-life balance also helps to avoid burnout and improves general wellbeing.

Develop compassion and empathy: Put yourself in other people's shoes and try to comprehend their viewpoints and experiences to develop empathy. Treating people with kindness and compassion may build better relationships and a more compassionate society.

Accept lifetime learning: Develop a mindset of constant learning and look for chances to advance personally and professionally. To increase your knowledge and abilities, attend seminars, online courses, or workshops.

Give back to society by participating in volunteer work or community service to positively impact your town.

Recall that personal development is an ongoing process and that every person's path is different. Select the areas that most speak to you, then set out on your journey of self-improvement with openness, curiosity, and commitment.

Of course! Here are some further suggestions to carry on with your quest for personal development and betterment:

Accept discomfort: Make it a habit to push yourself outside your comfort zone. Adopting a new approach, accepting a difficult assignment, or confronting a fear—embracing discomfort can increase potential and personal development.

Engage in self-compassion: Be kind, understanding, and forgiving to yourself. Acknowledge that errors are inevitable because you are a human. You may overcome disappointments and keep a great relationship with yourself by practicing self-compassion.

Develop your emotional intelligence by learning to recognize and understand both your own and other people's feelings. Making wiser judgments, handling disagreements, and navigating relationships are all aided by this ability.

Take regular breaks and rest: Make time for relaxation a priority in your daily self-care regimen. Allow yourself to rest and recover, improving your output, creativity, and general health.

Encourage a growth-oriented perspective: Adopt a mentality that welcomes difficulties, views setbacks as teaching moments, and has faith in the capacity for improvement. Adopting a growth mindset makes it possible to make improvements over time.

Examine your interests and passions: Allocate time for pursuits and interests that make you happy and fulfilled. In addition to being enjoyable, participating in activities you're passionate about promotes self-expression and self-discovery.

Develop an attitude of thankfulness by routinely recognizing and appreciating the good things in your life. This exercise helps you focus on your successes and encourages an optimistic outlook.

Establish appropriate limits in both your personal and professional lives. Establish clear boundaries and prioritize your needs to keep a healthy balance and safeguard your well-being.

Gain efficient time management skills: You may increase your output and efficiency by mastering efficient time management strategies. Set priorities for your job, eliminate distractions, and make a plan that will allow you to work with intention and attention.

Create coping strategies, develop a positive mindset, and draw lessons from prior setbacks to build resilience. You can overcome obstacles and hardship and preserve your mental and emotional health by being resilient.

Develop your active listening abilities to help you communicate more effectively. Pay close attention to the person speaking, try to grasp their viewpoint, and then thoughtfully answer. Relationships are strengthened, and good communication is promoted by active listening.

Develop a positive outlook on failure: Reframe your failure as a chance for personal development and education. Accept setbacks as stepping stones to achievement and use them as inspiration to keep going and get better.

Take part in self-care activities: Schedule time for mental, physical, and spiritual nourishment. This can involve walking outdoors, doing yoga or meditation, engaging in a favorite pastime, or taking a soothing bath.

Think about your values: Give your basic beliefs some thought and clarity. Your decisions, actions, and priorities will be guided by your understanding of what is genuinely important to you, resulting in a more authentic and fulfilling existence.

Honor and celebrate your accomplishments: Regardless of how big or small, take a minute to recognize and honor your accomplishments. Celebrating accomplishments gives you more self-assurance, strengthens constructive habits, and inspires you to keep improving.

Recall that personal development is an ongoing process. Select the concepts that speak to you and make them a part of your everyday existence. Make it a constant goal to better yourself, and approach the process of self-improvement with tolerance, tenacity, and self-compassion.

Section 1

New York is experiencing brutally hot days in June.

The long stone path leading to the school entrance leads to New York High School, situated by the river.

Kate has been here for two days now. The people with me talked about going to a tiny grocery store to get some everyday necessities to stock the vacant dorm.

Kate is unable to accompany them.

As she wasn't given a dormitory assignment.

This high school's volunteer teacher dormitory is a row of dilapidated red brick structures with precisely six rooms. One of the rooms was inundated and unusable due to the previous night's intense rain.

It was necessary to fix the walls and windows as well.

She was the last one to get into the dorm. When she got there, she discovered the room was occupied.

However, the three girls refused to allow her to live with them.

Nobody wanted to give in because the room was crowded and cramped, and nobody knew the girls.

Kate is not one to compete; everyone dutifully follows the plans. The principal promised to come up with a solution right away.

New York is in a rural location, the economy is struggling, and it essentially struggles to attract and keep talent. A unique group of teachers who cleared the test two years ago came to this place, stayed for no more than three months, and departed.

There is a severe teacher shortage at the school right now. They had no choice but to depend on these college students to come serve as volunteer teachers until a group of special teachers arrived.

After joking and chatting, they left Kate alone in the office.

The only sound coming from outside the window was the chirping of cicadas; sometimes, a breeze would blow through it, sending heat waves into the room.

Kate's skin flushed, and her forehead was sweaty due to the extreme heat.

She got up and started to turn on the electric fan after glancing around and realizing it was on the table.

She fiddled with it briefly before realizing the electric fan was broken.

She had no choice but to take a seat.

"Mistress Kate." "Let's eat some watermelon to cool down first. The electric fan is broken. The weather is too hot," the principal said, hurrying in and setting half a watermelon on the table.

This forty-year-old principal of a New York high school has her hair tucked in a tidy knot and is dressed in a polished black outfit.

With a fairly friendly smile, she continued, "Eat. We'll talk while we eat."

What else is there to discuss? At the moment, the focus is mostly on the dorm. "Our school is by the river; almost no one lives nearby; Mrs. Eva in town is the closest and most convenient way," someone said.

"I just spoke with Mrs. Eva, and she welcomes you. She lives alone, and the house is frequently empty of rooms.

The principal took a long time to decide on this.

Currently, this is the best answer that comes to mind.

The principal stopped speaking, and Kate listened patiently.

"Will it bother you at home, I wonder?"

She didn't anticipate letting her go to a different house; initially, she assumed she would offer her a room at the school.

Since they were all strangers when she arrived, she was terrified to trespass into other people's houses.

"No." "Mrs. Eva is very nice," said the principal with a smile.

Kate said nothing at all and fell silent.

"Teacher Kate, I understand your worries." Seeing Kate's tentative demeanor, the school principal said right away.

This time, there were a lot of volunteer teachers, and Kate stood out as the most abnormal of them all.

Her eyes are shaped like a new moon, her skin is immaculately white, and her smile brings people together. She is stunning. There is a soft and clean sound when speaking.

It's possible that the girl is spoiled and that the family is doing extremely well.

He did, however, consent to visit them as a volunteer teacher.

"I'll take you to see it this afternoon, then decide," the principal stated.

Kate said with a nod, "Yes."

from the classroom to Mrs. Eva needed fifteen minutes or so.

In the middle is a two-meter-wide stretch of crushed stone-paved road that is difficult to walk on and rarely has any traffic.

The path is uneven and rocky.

"This road is difficult to travel, even though it was repaired and paved more than ten years ago."

When the principal noticed that Kate was having trouble walking, she slowed down and gave her the advice, "Be careful."

After glancing down at her feet, Kate cast a questioning glance around.

The landscape of New York is breathtaking.

Vegetable fields, fruit trees, and little yards constructed by the families themselves may be found on the side of the road, which winds around a vast green mountain.

"Arrived."

Kate lifted her head, following the voice. All she could see with her eyes was a line of fences. Old red bricks encircle the wall on all sides, and the one-story house has flowers planted in the corners; everything is quite orderly.

After guiding Kate inside, the principal loudly screamed, "Mrs. Eva, are you home?" and banged on the door.

"Hey, come on over here." A reply came from within, the door opened, and Mrs. Eva hurriedly left.

She had a smile on her face and exuded a very kind and kind demeanor. "Mrs. Clover, I just killed a chicken," she said, smiling after bending her head to dry her hands. Tonight, let's stay put and enjoy dinner together."

The largest ritual in their tiny towns and villages to greet guests is the killing of ducks and hens. It's all a result of their excellent nutrition and hard work as parents raising them.

"Is Kate the teacher here?" Keeping an eye on the individual sitting close to the principal, Mrs. Eva said, "Come in here quickly and sit."

Mrs. Eva is a warm and welcoming person. In addition to the two sentences she consented to, the principal informed her that she wanted to transfer Kate here for a while this morning.

Since the town's kids also needed to treat the teachers with respect, their daughter consented to come to work for them as a teacher.

In addition, she had an empty room and lived alone.

"Teacher Kate intends to move here when? I only learned today that you are going to cook a chicken tonight!

Kate wasn't exactly used to such enthusiasm. She wanted to say "hello, Mrs. Eva" for a little second while she was in shock, but her voice rang out first.

You don't have to be concerned about upsetting her. She is by herself. She still wants a partner, on the other hand. Generally speaking, speaking is beneficial.

"Leave me show you the room," I said. As she led folks inside to observe, Mrs. Eva spoke.

The house has three rooms in total; two of them are unoccupied, and one is inside with a locked door. Mrs. Eva mentioned that her grandson occasionally visited the house.

"The room is extremely clean; she has already cleaned it."

It was lying next to the flower pot in the yard when Mrs. Eva brought her to view it. She could see it as soon as she opened the window. The living area includes an additional electric fan. The entire space is elegantly blue and cozy. I will retrieve it for you.

"Great wind, cool as promised!"

It is unbearably hot outside right now without an electric fan.

"Teacher Kate, please rest assured here," remarked Mrs. Eva.

Kate concurs.

You head back to the school office to pack your belongings after Kate leaves Mrs. Eva.

Not much needed to be cleaned up because a few individuals had returned.

"Kate, I just noticed the group message. Have you secured housing yet?"

Conveniently positioned on the table, TuongBoiBoi's hand held a huge plastic bag that she had recently purchased from the grocery.

"Um, the school principal is looking for help," Kate said, nodding.

"We were just chatting with the owner of the supermarket." Here, we learned of some mayhem. Allow me to explain."

TuongBeiBoi is gregarious and enjoys conversing with strangers wherever he goes.

"This New York appears to be serene and pleasant, but the most bothersome thing is that there appears to be a scoundrel who appears to go by the last name Smith."

"Fighting and causing trouble, oppressing the weak, there is no evil thing left undone, bad reputation resounds."

"The landlady keeps telling us that even though this town is a little larger than usual, we would run across him. It's better to exercise caution and not agitate him, or else it's over."

Following his remarks, TuongBoiBoi said, "But he is currently going to school in the district, so he probably won't be back for the time being."

She spoke something, and Kate answered with a few sentences but showed no interest in what she said.

TuongBeiBoi's head shifted to stare as his face became hot.

Ho Du, seated behind, gave her a look that suggested he wanted her to keep asking.

"Kate, did you know we might still need to be in homeroom this time?"

After some talking, the subject eventually returned to its original theme.

She wanted to ask this question.

Section Four

I picked up my car keys and cleaned my electronics when I returned to work.

I ran to my car, growing increasingly uncomfortable by the minute. It worsened as I stepped outside into the bright sunshine and brisk breeze. I could feel all the nooks and crannies the Coke had gotten into as it dried and adhered the fabric to my skin.

I took my simple black T-shirt out of my luggage and opened the trunk of my automobile. The shirt wasn't even that great—it was just a plain tee with a few holes here and there and some fading from repeated washings—because I had intended to go over to the project house after work, as is my usual routine. Luckily, Booms and Nibbles had a relatively laid-back clothing code. I had forgotten to pack a bra to change into, so

I couldn't spend the entire day in this one.

Befriending the brand manager and working for a lingerie company has some unexpected advantages. Angela would not object if I took a bra from her fitting room.

Booms and Nibbles concentrated on specialist sizing, so it took me some time to find one in my size, but I did find one. Regretfully, it had a lot of padding and gel wedges in the bottom of the cup. I had never worn anything like this and was comfortable with my chest despite being on the smaller side, hardly a B.

Desperate circumstances.

I would at least have the restroom to myself because everyone would be in the meeting. My only option was to undress and use damp paper towels to wipe my chest. I changed bras in the restroom first so as not to fully expose myself, and then while standing at the sink without a shirt on, I tried my best to remove the stickiness. I giggled at my excessive amount of cleavage after holding my long hair back over my shoulders to check out the new bra while looking up at my mirror. I hoped no one would realize my girls had grown by nearly two sizes.

After putting on the T-shirt, I examined myself. With my tight pants and the gold necklace I wore, it didn't look half bad—almost like an upscale damaged T-shirt that cost much too much.

Before Angela had all the fun, it was time to hurry to the meeting. She was probably drooling over the conference room table right now.

Since the meeting was probably almost over, I didn't bother to get my phone or iPad and instead went to the conference room, carefully opening the door. It had not worked to slip in, though. Everybody in the room looked at me. With indifference, most of them quickly returned their focus to the front of the room while Tessa simply grinned at me. When your employer isn't upset that you skipped most of the meeting, that's always a plus.

Standing close to Tessa, the new guy at the front just seemed relieved to see me. Angela looked at me for a moment, furrowing her brows. Slowly, she tipped her head to one side, then the other, and her mouth fell open, widening her eyes.

Of course. I should have realized it would be her who would notice my chest. She most likely believed I had done it intentionally to attract the new guy's interest. She had no idea that I had previously captured his interest far more compellingly. I let out a choked laugh. I looked across the room and put my hand over my lips in horror. Sure enough, I had the whole group's attention once more.

Coughing, I hastily sat down.

That's it for now, everyone. Tessa remarked, "I hope everyone will support Adam wholeheartedly. "Thank you for coming; that's all I have."

Alright, I feel silly right now. Before the conference concluded, I had only been seated for twenty seconds.

I remained in my seat while everyone else stood up and went. I was clueless as to why. Perhaps to lessen the ridiculousness of my initial decision to sit down?

The new guy and Tessa backed off and approached me. It's time to get up.

Tessa said, "Adam told me what happened." "At least you had a change of clothes."

I tugged at my shirt's hem. "But it's kind of scrubby."

It's alright, Tessa remarked. "And since you could meet Adam alone, I suppose you didn't need to attend the meeting anyway."

I smiled at him. Until then, he had been silently standing next to Tessa, and even though I had deliberately kept my eyes on Tessa, I could feel him observing me. "Since we didn't exchange names, I wouldn't call it a meeting." I extended my right hand toward him. My name is Rian Stratford.

Shaking my hand, he said, "Adam Jeong."

Tessa replied, "Well, I have another meeting." "Adam, thanks for coming along. I'm excited to collaborate with you.

He watched her go for a while before turning his black gaze back to me and said, "Thank you for the opportunity." Alright, Rian. You were going to explain how I could make you feel better.

"After considering it, I've decided you should take me to dinner."

He gave me a blink. "Eat dinner?"

I tried to look calm as I smiled at him. I'd long since figured out that the easiest way to avoid a guy freaking out when I approached him first was to appear relaxed. Yes. It's far more fun than paying to have my blouse dry cleaned, but not much more. Just a notion.

I held my breath and relaxed my shoulders while he thought about it. He nodded after pressing his lips together thoughtfully. "Let's carry it out. I'm busy setting up shop and relocating, but if you can wait until Friday, that would be great.

Not at all. That is ideal. It's a date, then.

He seems taken aback by my word choice but not angry. He chewed the inside of his lower lip, then gently let go. Even though I couldn't fully interpret his expression, he was all the more alluring for his mystery. He nodded at the end and added, "I'll be in touch." Rian, am I correct?

"You're capable."

With a nod, he exited the room. I gave a triumphant wiggle to my hips and pumped my fist once I was positive he was gone. I returned to my workstation, practically floating on air with delight.

However, my chair was already taken when I arrived.

Angela squinted her eyes at me as she looked up from her phone. "You were dishonest."

I threw back my head in shock. I had invited Adam out, but she was unaware of it. "What are you discussing?"

She gestured to my chest. "The bra you're wearing is padded."

I chuckled while prodding the gel inserts. "You observed."

"Girl, I see all of the boobs. It's what I do. And while it may not appear perfect, you cheated, in my opinion. She gestured to her smooth chest. "You knew that even with a padded bra, I couldn't compete."

In reality, I didn't mean to do it. Before the meeting, Adam and I ran into each other in the hallway, and his Coke splattered all over me. I took this bra out of your sample room because mine got drenched. That this was the only one you had in my size is not my fault.

"You collided with him? You are very lucky, man.

"You mean bad luck."

"Heh.Untruths. You're happy that it happened, you know. Take a look at you. You seem enthusiastic about something. She gasped and paused. "Are you telling me that he asked you out already?"

"No." I gave a playful smile. "I made a date request to him. Please get off of my seat now. It seems that I have to get to work, unlike you.

Angela got to her feet, but she kept looking at me. "You are amazing, girl. I'll even let you retain the bra because I'm such a good buddy, so he won't be wondering how you shrank the next time he sees you.

I shrugged, not giving a damn. "He had seen me before, my shirt stuck to my chest like a Coke blob. Furthermore, I don't believe he's the kind to focus on it.

Rian, hurry up. That kind of person is all guys. Enjoy your only date, then. To position myself as the obvious next step, I will schedule as many meetings with him as I can in the interim.

I tried not to let her mocking get to me, but as she walked away, I stuck my tongue out at her. She was also mistaken. Between now and Friday night, I was going to break this curse of the first kiss—even if it meant killing myself—so there was no way I was going to turn down a second date.

Bryce 2

I won't stay at this fitness center with that insane woman. I quickly finished my final set, cleaned the equipment, and headed out the door.

Even though I'm annoyed that the stranger judged me immediately, I feel satisfied that she was ultimately the driving force behind Denise and my reunion. Denise tries to hide her desire for me with a seductive lip bite, but it's obvious.

I'm eager to investigate this relationship, but I don't intend to cause my buddy Tiffany any problems. They've had a troubled past, and I don't want to be a part of it.

Denise was the first person I saw when I was in town for a job training more than a year ago. Denise stormed through and kicked Tiffany out of the hotel as if Tiffany wasn't dating the proprietor when I caught up with her. I never found out the whole story, but if Denise tossed weight like that, there had to be a significant issue.

All I know is that Tiffany and her soon-to-be husband were just getting started at the time. Denise has been stuck in my head ever since. I tried to get my shot, but when she didn't react, I figured she was already gone.

I'm not sure what the deal is right now.

I decided to stop at the front desk instead of going straight to my room, hoping that Denise would be there, but she wasn't.

I leave her employee a message. "Tell her that I expressed my gratitude earlier."

She says, "If you want to talk to her, I can call her back."

I'm not going to show up here looking petty. I can only imagine how chaotic things will get for Denise once the wedding, which is later today, gets underway.

I read her name tag and turned down her offer. "Isabella. Lovely name. No, Isabella, thank you. I'm sure you'll convey the word to her. I give her a short wave, knock twice on the desk, and reach the elevators.

I put my headphones back on and listen to the music while I wait for the elevator. I am excited but anxious about starting something crazy and unplanned with Denise.

Finally, the doors opened, and I strolled inside to see my reflection in the mirrored walls. I pause to smooth out my goatee and adjust my locs.

Tiffany has a packed travel itinerary, so her wedding is at the very end. I needed a vigorous workout to control the stress that was beginning to show on my face. It was not made easier by that guest.

By the time I return to the room, it is still early. I change into my underwear as soon as I enter and enjoy the nice air conditioning, hoping that the towels I asked for before heading to the gym have been replenished by housekeeping. I don't want to wait to take a hot shower.

I turn the corner to enter the restroom and immediately approach Denise. I instinctively reach out to grab her to avoid tipping her over. As I draw her in closer, she speaks up. My noise-canceling headphones muffle her. I remove them while continuing to hug her.

"Your penis," she yells.

Only then do I even consider that I'm standing there, nude, my dick pressed up against her thigh.

"Oh my god, sh*t. I apologize. I release her and cover my manhood with my hands.

She lets go of my used towels and looks away. "I apologize; I was only changing the towels. I need a housekeeper badly.

That clarifies her presence here. I consider everyday housekeeping to be wasteful, so I frequently skip it. Although I don't require new sheets daily and can make my bed, I always ask them to change the towels first thing in the morning.

"I had no idea that anyone was in here. Still cupping myself, I tell her, "I had my headphones on." I search for extra clothing to cover up so she'll feel at ease turning around.

She reached for the towels, and I reached down for one at the same moment. Each of us lets go, then reaches back for them.

I say, "Go ahead."

Not at all. You must have one.

Yes, but those are filthy, too.

Horrible. Apologies. She slants forward to grab them.

"Where is the cart?" I query her.

What kind of cart?

"During room service, don't you guys have a housekeeping cart or something?"

Yes, but I was only there to change your towels. For that, I don't need a cart. She looks up at me.

Her gaze moves to my hands, covering my dick. She turns her head quickly as she realizes she's been stared at, and I clear my throat. "I have to leave."

With her eyes dropped to avoid my gaze, Denise passes past me. She dashes out of the room, and I laugh.

She disappears out of sight as the door closes, leaving me stunned and wondering if we could have continued the conversation in a different direction.

***

In contrast to the last several hours, work often takes up most of my time and attention. My commitment to my work has come at the expense of my personal life throughout the last five years. Most ladies I meet find it difficult to understand that I'm not seeking a committed relationship. They act as though they have no problems with having sex, yet it always ends badly. They constantly believe they are the ones who will persuade me otherwise. Not because I'm interested, but I never stay in one area long enough for a relationship.

Denise diverts my attention. She is a mystery, a riddle that I cannot solve. And because I'm a man who enjoys a good challenge, her mystery draws me in. I would like to know every detail about her.

Not to mention, all of the traveling I've done in the last few months has left me feeling backed up and sexually irritated. In the last six months, I have visited four other states, and old contacts fell through in all four of them. There's just one way to get rid of her level of mental encroachment. I have to finish something quickly. I try working one free in the shower, but it just makes me crave the real thing more.

BeforeBefore the wedding, I tried to finish a little work. I put my headphones back on and lose myself in a concentration zone. Time flies by in an instant.

My parents were heavy laborers, so I always could lose myself in thought and concentrate for protracted amounts of time. I've advanced in my company so rapidly because of that. I can work from anywhere and pick my hours because I'm one of the best engineers. I want to play harder even while I work hard.

It's time to have fun at this wedding now that the work is finished.

At first, I was hesitant to attend. I dated Tiffany in high school a very long time ago. To be honest, I was trying to find out what she was on when I was in town more than a year ago. Drama has never been my thing, so when I found out she was married and having an affair with James, I immediately distanced myself. Even though I was first hesitant to be here, I'm now very delighted for them both.

Before this gets rolling, I walk down early to grab a beer or something. The floor under mine is where the elevator stops. Denise entered wearing a stunning blue dress that fit her figure perfectly. The stress I managed to release earlier returns. Although my expression doesn't reflect it, I'm drooling over her like that cartoon dog with his tongue and eyeballs sticking out.

The material reveals toned legs that go on for days as it falls just above her knee. Her back is covered in loose curls that resemble a dark chocolate waterfall. I can't stop staring at her; she seems so beautiful.

She is more complex than her outward seems, though. Denise possesses beauty and power, which combine to create a potent combination. I can't help but be pulled to her, curious to learn more about this poised, strong woman.

The curve of her lips and the warmth in her gaze catch my attention as she turns to face me. It's contagious, and I can't help but see my lips moistening in reaction. Her face lights up with a smile that extends to her eyes. I knew then that I wanted to be the one to bring that kind of joy to her face every day.

Denise teases, "Mr. Miller, it's nice to see you dressed."

I frantically try to stop my eyes from examining her physique in that dress, saying, "Call me Bryce." Hello, I apologize for this earlier. I didn't intend to come across to you in that way.

"It's just a dick," she answers as if it were all unimportant.

Oh no. Though, damn, I'm glad she's not insulted.

"Did you enjoy the remainder of your training?" Moving on as if she hadn't just damaged my ego, she asks.

"It wasn't too bad."

"All right?" With a note of disappointment in her tone, Denise inquires. "I apologize if our facilities fell short of your expectations."

"It's simply a gym," I reply.

She chuckles as she realizes my tone of mockery.

She is biting her lower lip once more.

I let myself get lost in the here and now, wondering what it would be like to take her in this elevator by hiking that skirt up. See for yourself what that clothing is hinting at. Observing our image in the many mirrors that surround us.

"Is there any way I can surpass your expectations?" I inquire, advancing closer to her with a seductive look. I get up excited.

She gathers herself and exits when the elevator chimes.

"I'll see you at the wedding, Mr. Miller," she responds in a polished voice.

I must get over whatever is between us quickly to avoid blowing up.

As I approached the bar, I noticed Denise working hard to prepare for the nuptials. She's taking the lead, assigning assignments to her group, and organizing every aspect to guarantee perfection. Denise moves calmly and collectedly around the room.

Seeing her in action makes me even more attracted to her if I wasn't already. She is confident without coming across as hostile. Sensual without making an effort. She has an amazing manner about her that conveys competence and confidence. Nonetheless, she has a vulnerability in her eyes that is quite telling.

And then there's her contagious smile that makes my heart skip a beat. I want to be the one to laugh with her, to make her smile, and to share her secrets with her. She is like an unread book. I can't help but want to turn the pages to learn more about her. For now, I'm content with watching her from afar.

Seated in a small chamber near the BSF border gate at Hussainiwala, Kundan was in complete astonishment. At first, the BSF officer didn't think Kundan's amazing narrative could be true. As the officer watched Kundan sob uncontrollably, he concluded that Kundan was most likely insane. But when Kundan regained emotional control and began speaking more clearly, the officer became more and more certain that Kundan's story was real.

After that, the officer began to treat him seriously, and his superiors were consulted on the situation. When the bosses saw how serious the situation was, they began questioning Kundan. He begged them, bringing to their notice that he was a well-known businessman from Mumbai with an unparalleled reputation.

It was unclear to Kundan if his father had purposefully jumped into the river or had lost his balance and tumbled off the hill. The idea that a 76-year-old guy would willingly jump into a river was absurd. However, after embarking on this peculiar adventure, he could no longer be positive about anything. Immediately after, a search party was sent to find "the old man who had either fallen off the mound or jumped off it."

Kundan's head was suddenly filled with an idea. Was there a chance his father had killed himself? It dawned on him that his father had discussed the newspaper articles before he fell into the river. A knot formed in his throat as remorse overcame him for bothering his father with the stories from the newspaper. Did their recent separation reach its peak with this incident? He buried his face in his hands in helplessness as more tears flooded his eyes.

The lengthy and torturous interrogation would have tested even the most seasoned criminal. Despite their uncertainty over how to handle Kundan, the BSF officers did not report the issue to higher authorities after carefully evaluating the circumstances. He was requested to remain back by the BSF until more details about his father could be obtained.

Without thinking, he reached into his pocket for a cigarette and lighted it. These days, he stayed away from smoking, but circumstances required it. Kundan puffed up and wrapped his arms tightly around his coat to protect himself from the chilly early morning air. Suddenly realizing that this was his father's cloak that he had been wearing all along, he felt something firm press against his tummy. He had no idea what had happened during the last three hours; it had been quite the roller coaster. Putting his hand inside the coat pocket out of reflex, he discovered three hardback black diaries that were tatty but held together with a rubber band.

He reasoned it would be appropriate to go to the authorities and give them the journals. In the next instant, he had second thoughts. He was sorely tempted to read the journals since his curiosity overcame him. He moved from the BSF office where he had been questioned and sat on the bench outside. It was nearly enough light in the early morning to read the diary. He turned to the first page and read a few of the lines.

I have never thought of keeping a journal before in my life. I must admit that I was never very bold, but I've always believed that a diary is for people who dare to face the truth. But recent experiences in my life have forced me to think back on the past. I no longer think about life in the same way as I did before these experiences. They have given me confidence that I would never have imagined gaining, and they have inspired me to walk a route paved with harmony and serenity (the kind that would bring about the peace that the mind so desperately seeks) and paved with conflicts and challenges.

Imperfections are often accentuated in retrospect, and I admit I had many of them throughout my life. The heart wants nothing but redemption in the somber calm of the evening when life's illusions become apparent. However, remorse never stops trying to torment the mind, and no matter what you want, the consequences always seem to loom enormous. I felt compelled, therefore, to summarize the extraordinary experiences that have shaped me and altered my life irrevocably.

Kundan closed his eyes and inhaled deeply as though bracing himself for the magnitude of the moment he was about to experience. What looked like a report of the truth he was looking for was in his hands. His father's flowing and vivid descriptions transported him to a world he could never have imagined, and as he read the diary, his heart started to race.

Chapter 1 Skye

My flowing onyx crystal robe shimmers in the silvery moonlight, hiding my footprints as the stars softly dance across the night clouds.

Magnificence drapes my feet, and the Crown of Diamonds rests atop my head, unattainable by anyone.

With my most faithful retainers, Rufus and Logan, encircling me in their exquisite silk robes, I tiptoe toward my lofty crystal throne, my opulent grace adorning each step.

The Council stands up to celebrate my beautiful arrival. At my command, thousands of brave troops are prepared to face the largest assault in history. They are holding arms in my honor.

"Under my kind supervision, humanity has polluted my universe for an extended period. My generosity has come to an end. I am the one bringing the Apocalypse, and it is here. The sky is me. The planet will quake beneath me when I unleash mayhem and complete catastrophe. I am Skye, Queen of the New Order.

The throne hall erupts in triumphal cheers. Now, there's no turning back.

My Army General Kristoff bows and says, "The troops await your command, My Queen."

"All right, General, start the countdown. Prepare the North Gate for our impending attack. We don't spare any victims.

"Your Majesty, yes."

"Humanity's sins of filth and bile will not be forgiven. Now, they'll recognize me for who I truly am.

I hold back.

"For whom ought they to?" I say it again, bringing the manuscript up to my face. This is 'for whom they should,' isn't it? I ask my audience of one woman.

"You believe that as well?" she asks.

Ahh. Alright, this is enough for me.

I break free from my ruthless, obsessed retribution Queen of the Universe persona for a brief period. Let's get back to reality.

The reality is set in a bed and breakfast reception area where I work, not in the opulent Crystal Palace of a resident Evil Queen with intentions to subjugate the entire planet.

"Darla, may I tell you the truth?"

Darla scoffs. "What awful dialogue?"

The worst, I declare. "Why did you allow this to occur?"

Darla grunts in exasperation and digs her fingers into her hair.

She describes herself as a "seasoned" screenwriter! This was not what I was expecting—bland. It's my fault for being lazy.

I adore Darla Owens dearly, but this is not acceptable at all. She was paired with Tina Hawkins for a class assignment to co-write an apocalyptic scene.

This joke is catastrophic.

I recall being ecstatic when she told me about her idea and that she wanted to name the antagonist after me.

However, it seems like everything fell apart after Tina joined the team.

"Well, the idea was brilliant, and the plot is fantastic, but this script ruins all your hard work. It's said that Queen Skye is a fierce antagonist for whom we all have a hidden admiration.

Indeed! A gorgeous femme fatale, full of narcissism, Darla says. "This entire show is devoid of that. At this rate, I'm going to receive a failing grade.

I wholeheartedly concur. For this reason, group assignments in college are the scourge of our existence. "You ought to speak with Tina and perhaps work out a compromise. This is not at all what you were envisioning.

Darla sighs, "She changed everything, and I just let her." Could you imagine that Logan and Rufus were meant to be enormous, snow-white, saber-toothed tigers?

"Oh my goodness, that would have been magnificent! Why did she alter that?

"She believes it to be cliche."

"Cliché? Has she perused this? I ask, emphasizing with a hand up of the manuscript. "Here's my advice: get her off the screenplay and focus entirely on your story. She should consider a small scenario and include it in the film. Or you could find a new companion.

"No, it's too late to find another person. We'll just wing it. This is all the fault of Professor Collins and his obnoxious idea of fishing.

I taunt, "Imagine he takes all your ideas and turns them into some major Hollywood hit."

We'll probably tear him to pieces. No forgiveness."

Darla and I have been pals since I first entered Thackeray College through the ancient metal gates. Her purple fringed hair and how she wore her sass on her sleeves had drawn my attention. After conversing, we shared a room for our first academic year. Fun times.

Since we no longer live together, our connection is maintained by late-night texting and video conversations when I'm not assisting her with practicing monologues or editing manuscripts.

We won't get to see one other in person too often now that the holidays are over. Since Darla is a Media and Communications major and I attend the School of Business, there is very little likelihood that we will cross paths on campus.

Darla is also a well-known reporter for Thackeray's broadcasting outlet, The Daily Bugle—what I refer to as a glorified Press Club. Even on the weekends, she becomes just as engrossed in her work as I do. Thus, spending time together like this is unusual, and it has been going on for at least five hours.

"It's incredibly late." I should return to my work now. I declare.

Yes, but what fun is that going to be? I have a superior concept. Darla smiles.

"Darla, I've already lost enough brain cells reading Tina's script."

"Cancel the script. Have a drink with me.

"What do we celebrate?" With renewed zeal, I inquire. "Avoid referring to the patriarchy's demise."

Darla gives me a shot glass from the minibar while giggling. "I always drink to that, you know that. However, this one is for a new semester, when you, Skye, will have to coexist with people you don't like and be separated from what you most enjoy doing, which is managing this facility.

Chapter 3: Unhappiness Unveiled

Emma's dissatisfaction with her connection with Imprint had been growing like an unstoppable wave that was hard to ignore. That night, her unanswered concerns and unfulfilled desires weighed upon her as she stayed on the oceanfront.

Emma noticed that the stars were beginning to twinkle in the dimming sky. Her heart heavy with the realization that her once-enthused ambitions were now antiquated relics of the past, she gazed out at the endless ocean.

She thought back to when she first started dating Imprint, the butterflies in her stomach, and her intense desire to find love. However, as of late, their fondness had evolved into something pleasant almost daily. She had experienced enough shocks, unrestrained encounters, and, most importantly, passionate kisses that made her heart race.

"Is this all there is?" she whispered to the breeze, but her words fell short of her lips.

Her friends often resented her consistent relationship with Imprint, but Emma couldn't get rid of the feeling that she was missing out on something more meaningful, something that would make her feel alive again. She longed for an organization founded on comfort, commonality, and devotion that would ignite her spirit.

Emma's dissatisfaction deepened over time, straining her relationship with Imprint. She knew she should talk to him about these feelings, but the thought of hurting him was very heavy on her mind. To her dismay, destiny had other plans. She was to have an opportunity experience that would force her to confront her desires and ultimately guide her toward an adoration that was as surprising as it was enthusiastic.

The Innocence of Childhood

The first chapter of "The Journey of the First Kiss" begins on a warm sunny afternoon in the small, picturesque town of Littlerock. This was the town where everyone knew everyone else, where life was simple and full of innocent charm. Within this idyllic setting, we're introduced to our protagonists - a vibrant, freckle-faced girl named Jane and a shy, dreamy-eyed boy named David.

Jane and David were seven years old and lived on the same street, just a few houses apart. With her bright green eyes and wild, curly hair, Jane was the kind of child who could turn anything into an adventure. She was brave, outgoing, and full of energy. Her laughter was contagious, and her spirit was infectious. David, on the other hand, was quiet and thoughtful. He had a kind heart and a curious mind. He loved reading and could often be found with his nose buried in a book. He was content to sit and watch the world go by, taking in the small details others often missed.

Despite their contrasting personalities, Jane and David became fast friends. They spent countless hours together, exploring the neighborhood, playing make-believe, and sharing secrets. They were just children, yet their bond was strong and pure. This chapter paints a beautiful picture of their friendship, laying the foundation for the deeper relationship that would blossom in the coming years.

One defining incident in this chapter is when Jane, in her typical adventurous spirit, decides to climb the town's largest tree - an old, towering oak. Despite David's warnings, she scrambles higher and higher until she's just a speck against the vast blue sky. However, as she reaches for a particularly elusive branch, she loses her footing and falls;

David, watching in horror from below, rushes to her aid.

Jane escapes with a scraped knee and a bruised ego, but the incident leaves a lasting impact. David's worry for her safety, his tender care as he patches up her wound, and his gentle admonishment reveal a deeper affection. Jane, for her part, is touched by David's concern, and although she dismisses it with a laugh, it's clear that the incident has brought them even closer.

Despite being adventurous, Jane learns to appreciate David's cautious and considerate nature. She begins to see strength in his quietness and wisdom in his thoughtfulness. On the other hand, David finds himself captivated by Jane's fearless spirit and vibrant energy. He cherishes her laughter and the way her eyes light up when she talks about her dreams and adventures.

As the summer stretches, they share countless little moments - from chasing fireflies in the twilight to sharing stories under the starlit sky. One memorable event occurs at the annual town fair, where Jane coaxes a reluctant David onto the Ferris wheel. It's a magical scene - the twinkling lights, the view of the entire town from above, the shared bag of cotton candy. David, who was initially scared, finds himself laughing with Jane, their hands brushing against each other's subtly.

Throughout these experiences, the narrative highlights the subtleties of their growing bond. The casual touch of hands, the lingering looks, and the shared smiles - these innocent interactions take on a profound significance in their journey toward the first kiss.

One evening, while watching the sunset together, Jane asks David a question that marks a turning point in their friendship: "David, do you think we'll always be friends?" David, caught off guard, fumbles for an answer. He looks at Jane, the fading sunlight illuminating her hopeful face, and replies, "I hope we'll be more than that."

This chapter ends with Jane's infectious laughter fading into the twilight, leaving a thoughtful David under the darkening sky. Although he does not fully understand the depth of his own words at that moment, it's clear that their friendship is evolving into something more that will eventually lead to the anticipated first kiss.

"I can't believe you did that!" Myles is laughing her butt off after hearing what happened at the nurse's office.

I was tempted to tell her and Serena all about it when I got home yesterday, but I wanted to say it in person to enjoy their reaction.

So I told them while waiting for our math teacher, and they weren't disappointed. Well, Myles didn't.

She finds the whole thing entertaining.

"You think he'll even the score?" Serena's eyebrows are knitted together in a frown. Unlike Myles, she doesn't think it's funny.

"Probably." I shrug, not even the least bit concerned. "But I'm not worried. I'm not afraid of him."

"Yeah. It's not like he's going to hurt you or anything," Myles agrees. "I mean, this is Dean we're talking about. He fools around a lot, but he's harmless."

That was what I thought, too—until he proved me wrong and ruined my life. So now, he's officially on my hate list.

Not that it's a long list. It's just him and maybe Kayla Chavez for calling my hair the "Sahara Desert" that I forgot to blow dry it once. While I'm already over Kayla's comment, I'm still mad about Dean's actions. Especially after he proudly refused to take accountability for his actions.

"Well, tough. I'm not apologizing again."

The nerve of that boy. Just thinking about it makes my anger rise back to the surface.

"Nice video, Finley. You showed the floor, which was the boss," Evan Puck yells from the back of the class, dragging our attention. His friends surrounding him laugh at his lame joke.

My cheeks turn pink, but I refuse to feel embarrassed. He's not the first one to bring up that mortifying TikTok video, and definitely not the last. Since this morning, I've already heard a few comments about it.

I still don't have the slightest idea who uploaded it. Myles told me that they're hiding under an anonymous account, the coward.

Whatever. All I have to do is pretend the whole thing doesn't faze me. That should be easy.

With a sweet smile, I say loudly, "Oh, like when you hit that glass door with your face multiple times last year? I still remember that. Everyone does."

That's not even a lie. I heard a group of guys referencing that incident a few weeks ago.

The rest of the class goes, "Oooh," while Evan's face turns bright red. Then he mutters a word that sounds exactly like "witch."

"That's a good one," Myles cackles.

Serena nods in agreement, giggling behind her hand.

Like, I'll never let jerks like Evan humiliate me publicly. I always get even.

So Dean Andrews better watch out.

****

You can do it. Act like nothing bothers you.

Squaring my shoulders, I trail after Myles and Serena, gripping my lunch tray like my life depended on it. I feel eyes on me as we make our way to our table, which is smack dab in the center of the cafeteria.

"You all right?" Serena asks as I take the seat across from her and Myles.

I force a toothy smile. "Never better."

"Ignore these nosy losers," Myles tells me, glaring at the group of girls staring at me from the next table.

Their eyes grow wide collectively before moving away. Myles can be scary when she wants to be.

"They'll move on to a new scandal soon enough. Don't worry about it," Serena comforts me as if I need it.

I shake my head. "I'm not worried. I'm—" Mortified? Catty? Intent on getting my revenge? "—fine. Just fine."

"Well, if you say so." But she doesn't look convinced.

Heck, I'm not even sure I sound convincing.

"Oh, look. It's your new mortal enemy," Myles announces, looking over her shoulder.

I follow the direction of her gaze, my eyes narrowing into slits.

Because there he is—Dean. He's with his friends, acting as if nothing happened. He didn't cause me any trouble.

As if he senses me staring at him, he meets my gaze. Then scowls as I wronged him.

Seriously, the nerve!

"Looks like the mortal enemy thing isn't one-sided," Serena observes.

"Seems like it," Myles laughs. She says, "Are you going to go over there and confront him?"

"And let these jerks record it for another viral TikTok video?" I scoff, taking a sip from my iced tea. "No, thanks." The Childhood of Innocence

"The Journey of the First Kiss" opens with a pleasant, sunny afternoon in Littlerock, a charming little town. Everyone knew everyone else in a town like this, and daily life was easygoing and endearingly uncomplicated. Our two main characters, quiet, dreamy-eyed lad David and vivacious, freckle-faced girl Jane, are first shown to us in this picture-perfect environment.

David and Jane, seven years old, lived a short distance apart on the same street. Jane was the youngster who could make anything into an adventure with her wild, curly hair and brilliant green eyes. She was fearless, gregarious, and energetic. Her spirit was contagious, and her laughter was contagious. David, however, remained silent and reflective. He was inquisitive and had a good heart. He was a voracious reader, frequently seen with his nose deep in a book. He was happy to observe the world around him, seeing the little things most people would miss.

Even though Jane and David had different personalities, they quickly grew close. Together, they explored the area, played pretend, and shared many hours of secrets. Even though they were still young, they had a deep and sincere friendship. This chapter depicts Their friendship well, laying the groundwork for a deeper bond to develop in the years to come.

One pivotal moment in this chapter is when Jane, ever the adventurer, chooses to scale the town's biggest tree, an ancient, towering oak. She climbs higher and higher in defiance of David's warnings until she is reduced to little more than a dot in the big blue sky. But when she reaches for a particularly elusive branch, she stumbles and falls, and David, horrified and looking on from below, comes to her rescue.

Although Jane gets away with only a skinned knee and a damaged ego, the episode has an effect that doesn't go away. A deeper affection is evident in David's concern for her safety, his patient care as he tends to her wound, and his kind reprimands. For her part, Jane acknowledges that the experience has made them even closer, even if she laughs it off. She is affected by David's care.

Even though she is the more daring of the two, Jane values David's caution and consideration. She realizes that his thinking and stillness are sources of strength and knowledge. David, meanwhile, is enthralled by Jane's lively energy and brave personality. He treasures her laugh, and her eyes shine when she shares her experiences and dreams.

They spend many small moments together throughout the summer, such as chasing fireflies in the dusk and telling stories beneath the stars. One particularly memorable incident happened at the yearly local fair when Jane reluctantly persuaded David to ride the Ferris wheel. The shared bag of cotton candy, the shimmering lights, and the aerial perspective of the entire town create a lovely scenario. After being afraid at first, David starts laughing with Jane as their hands lightly caress one other.

The story emphasizes the nuances of their developing relationship as they go through these situations. In the lead-up to the first kiss, seemingly insignificant exchanges like holding hands, exchanging glances, and grinning together are important.

Jane asks David a question that turns their friendship on its head one evening as they watch the sunset together: "David, do you think we'll always be friends?" Taken off guard, David struggles to think of a response. With the last of the daylight casting a hopeful shadow over Jane's face, he looks at her and says, "I hope we'll be more than that."

When the sun sets in this chapter, Jane's contagious laughter fades into the dusk, leaving David reflecting beneath the lowering sky. Their friendship is growing into something more that will ultimately lead to the much-anticipated first kiss, even though he is still not entirely aware of the profundity of what he is saying.

Section Two

"That's unbelievable that you did that!" Having heard what transpired at the nurse's office, Myles is laughing uncontrollably.

When I arrived home yesterday, I was tempted to tell her and Serena everything, but I wanted to say it face-to-face to see how they responded.

While waiting for our math teacher, I told them, and they did not disappoint me. Myles, however, didn't.

She finds the whole situation amusing.

Do you believe he will balance the score? Serena frowns, her eyebrows pulled together. In contrast to Myles, she finds it amusing.

"Probably." I shrug, not caring in the slightest. "Yet I'm not concerned. I have no fear of him.

Indeed. Myles concurs, saying, "It's not like he's going to hurt you." We are talking about Dean, after all. He plays around a lot, but he is not dangerous.

I also believed that, but he disproved me and destroyed my life. He's officially on my hate list as of right now.

Not that the list is long. It's just him and possibly Kayla Chavez for referring to my hair as the "Sahara Desert" after I neglected to blow dry it once. Even though I've moved past Kayla's remark, I'm still furious about Dean's actions. Especially after he arrogantly declined to accept responsibility for his deeds.

Alright, difficult. I won't apologize once more.

That boy's nerve. The very thought of it brings my rage back to the surface.

Evan Puck calls out from the back of the room, "Nice video, Finley. You showed the floor who was the boss." His pals around him chuckle at his cheesy joke.

My cheeks flush, but I can't bring myself to feel ashamed. He's not the first, and certainly not the last, to bring up that embarrassing TikTok video. I've already heard a few remarks on it since this morning.

I'm still not even close to knowing who uploaded it. Myles informed me that they were hiding behind the cowardly anonymous account.

Whatever. All I have to do is act as though I'm not bothered by the situation. That ought to be simple.

"Oh, like when you hit that glass door with your face multiple times last year?" I ask, grinning sweetly, and raise my voice. That's still what I recall. Everyone can.

It's not even a lie, that. A few weeks ago, I heard some guys talking about that incident.

Evan's face grows red as the class goes, "Oooh." Subsequently, he murmurs a word that precisely resembles "witch."

"Well done on that one," Myles chuckles.

Serena giggles behind her hand as she nods in agreement.

As if I'll ever allow morons like Evan to make me seem bad in public. I always come out on top.

Dean Andrews had best take note.

****

You're capable of it. Pretend nothing is bothering you.

I square my shoulders and follow Myles and Serena, holding onto my lunch plate as if it were my last. We walk to our table in the middle of the cafeteria, and I can feel eyes on us.

"Are you okay?" As I take the seat across from Serena and Myles, she asks.

I grit my teeth and smile. "Never the better."

Myles instructs me to "ignore these nosy losers," frowning at the girls observing me from the adjacent table.

Together, their eyes enlarge, and then they turn away. When Myles feels like it, she can be frightening.

"They'll find another scandal to focus on before long. As though I needed it, Serena reassures me, "Don't worry about it."

I give a headshake. "I'm not concerned. I'm—" Shocked? Cate? Are you planning to exact revenge on me? Okay. Perfectly alright.

"All right, if you say so." She doesn't appear persuaded, though.

I don't even know if I sound convincing.

"Oh, I see. Glancing over her shoulder, Myles declares, "It's your new mortal enemy."

Slits form in my eyes as I follow her direction of sight.

For there he is, Dean. Acting like nothing happened, he is with his pals as though he hadn't bothered me.

He meets my stare as if he senses me staring at him. Then, he frowned as if I had done anything wrong.

The nerve!

Serena remarks, "It seems like the mortal enemy thing isn't one-sided."

Myles chuckles, "It seems like it." "Are you going to go over there and confront him?" she asks me.

"Let these bastards film it for yet another wildly popular TikTok video?" I sneer and take a drink of my chilled tea. "Thanks, but no."

But I have to act immediately. But precisely what? Is stuff trash in his locker? That seems like a really bad concept. A revolting and abhorrent notion. I would throw up from the fragrance alone.

Oh no. The very thought of that makes me want to throw up.

Thus, it is not worth the hassle.

I whisper, my eyes still concentrating on the boy still frowning at me, "I'll have to think of another way."

Indeed. Not at all biased, Myles murmurs.

But I have to act immediately. But precisely what? Is stuff trash in his locker? That seems like a really bad concept. A revolting and abhorrent notion. I would throw up from the fragrance alone.

Oh no. The very thought of that makes me want to throw up.

Thus, it is not worth the hassle.

I whisper, my eyes still concentrating on the boy still frowning at me, "I'll have to think of another way."

Indeed. Not at all biased, Myles murmurs.

After a few weeks, I resumed working with Rachel and Marlow. Even though Nick and I were still flirting, we hadn't kissed yet, as I grumbled. It was driving me crazy, to be honest, since it was all I could think about. I wanted to jump on him and steal a kiss so badly.

We three played rock, paper, scissors for the dishes in the rear as the evening grew sluggish. I defeated Rachel's paper, but Marlow's scissors prevailed. I sensed eyes on me while cleaning out a big saucepan elbow-deep in suds.

When I glanced around, I saw Nick leaning on the counter where he had repeatedly trapped me. His smile had a cunning mixture. My arms began to leak everywhere, so I picked up a towel and began to pat them dry.

"Why are you in this place?" He was not talking, so I asked.

He moved away from the counter with ease and got closer to me in just two steps. He questioned me as if I had kept my birthday a secret, "Why didn't you tell me you had a birthday?"

I gave a shoulder shrug. It hadn't been a major issue. After taking me out to dinner, my parents treated me to a girl's night out at Marlow's.

Sincerely, I said, "I didn't think it mattered to you because it was a while ago."

He had a pained expression on his face. It would have been significant, he stated.

I said, "I apologize," since what else could I say? Although we do flirt, I knew he wouldn't treat me to a birthday meal or anything similar, so I didn't see the need to tell him.

Then something else changed on his face. Something I was uncertain about. A small amount of fear mixed with a small amount of joy. Whenever his hands weren't on me, it was difficult to read him. Even after all these months, we had never moved past a few semi-intimate touches and precisely two kisses, even though I could always see the heat in his eyes.

Though he didn't lift a finger, he wanted to reach out and touch me. He looked down at the floor, then back up at me. "Why did you keep your virginity a secret from me?"

Oh my god! Who would I have to murder? Rachel or Marlow? The only people who knew were them. Marlow. I recognized her immediately. Unless she instructed him to keep me safe, Rachel is overly protective. However, it was dubious.

I attempted to downplay it. "I didn't realize I had to let you know," I answered.

"That was a wise move," he stated, sounding serious.

I was confused when I stared at him. "Had anything changed?" I enquired.

He gave a shoulder shrug.

Sometimes, it was so hard to figure out this man. I don't understand why he seemed to doubt some aspects of myself when he was the one having fun when he had a girlfriend. I let out a deep, frustrated sigh. What are you saying, then? You realized that I'm a virgin. Therefore, you regret whatever it was that we did?

He glanced at me. He answered, "I didn't say that at all," but he didn't elaborate.

I questioned, "So why does it matter?"

His dark brown eyes went straight through me. "I never would have been so brazen."

My heart fell. He would not have dealt with me the same way. I moved a step closer, making very little space between us. I answered quietly, "That's one of the things I like." "I appreciate your leadership and expertise, as I lack these qualities."

The corners of his mouth lifted along with his eyes. "Well," he remarked.

Alright?

What good is it? Is it better that he takes the lead or that I'm a virgin? He could be so mysterious at times that it was driving me crazy. But instead of making me crazy, he put his lips over mine and kissed me till I passed out.

Nick departed after confirming that I could support myself, and I returned to the other dishes. He had me spellbound with one kiss, and the worst part was that I was left wondering when I would get another since it wasn't something he did frequently.

Marlow returned to the dessert fridge just as I was cleaning up. I had been contemplating how precisely I would wring her neck and when she would have time to speak with Nick.

I pushed my hands to my hips and muttered, "So." "You revealed my virginity to Nick?"

She fell to the ground with a cheesecake plate. Did Christ come back to inform you, Christ?

She had told him only moments before, and he had returned to me, making me want to chuckle. "Marlow! How come you would tell him that?

Her expression contorted as she struggled to formulate a response. It wasn't as though I was merely going to inform him. She responded, a little afraid of my reaction, "It was more of a...um...you wanted him to be your first."

"What?" I cried out. "How could you, oh my god?"

Her face tightened as she winced. "I apologize. I just assumed he wouldn't play games with you if he knew you were still a virgin. He would either leave you alone or boink you.

Still, in astonishment, I muttered, "Shit, Marlow." "I want him to behave the same way. I found that appealing about him. And I promise to wring your neck if he quits making out with me!

After flinching, Marlow grinned. She knew I was angry but also knew I wouldn't wring her neck. "All right, I'll correct. I'll let him know you're annoyed by his constant flirtation.

I gave her a fierce glance. And chuckled after that. "You dare not! I threatened to "wring your neck twice" as I flung the towel at her.

She picked up another dish while dodging the towel. She hurried out of the kitchen, saying, "I gotta get these out to the customers."

All I could do was chuckle at the circumstances. Upon completing my duty and retiring for the evening, I couldn't help but worry if our relationship would improve. Even while I enjoyed our flirting, I wished it would stop. I desired to have him as my first.

I worked with Nick again on a Saturday morning. Four days following Marlow's confession of my virginity to him. En route to town, I wondered if he would behave differently and what I should do to ensure he didn't stop things.

Nick gave me a tired smile as he opened the door. Yes! Dammit, things were supposed to be different!

"Hello," I whispered to myself as I passed him, threatening to kick him in the balls if he called me a child.

"Hello, Rory," he answered.

That had not altered, at least. I went to the rear and clocked in after taking my apron out of my locker. I headed straight to the rear and began removing the buffet plates. With a groan, I bent to retrieve the remaining dishes. I did not want him to behave any differently at all. He probably wouldn't touch me again, and now it would be embarrassing.

I sighed and got up, carrying a sack full of containers. However, I backed against something, and others surrounded me. I screamed, and the containers crashed with an absurdly loud sound as they fell to the ground.

"Nick!" I exclaimed. "You nearly gave me a heart attack!"

Sam hurried around the corner to inquire about everyone's well-being. However, as soon as he noticed us, his gaze shifted to Nick's arms encircling me, and he gently moved away, appearing to have disrupted something.

Nick reached out and put his hand on my ear. He murmured, "All that sighing was making me..." before cutting himself off and pushing his hips to my back.

Aurora to Earth! He was having an enormous erection, and I was ecstatic and unsure of what to say or do. I decided to just freeze and keep silent. Or take a breath.

A tiny laugh escaped his lips. He asked in jest, "Are you worried or excited?"

Well, I was both since he asked. Did he intend to have a sexual relationship with me? My girlie parts tingled, and my tummy turned around.

Three: What's the Appropriate Time?

Never hurry.

You can contribute to the scene by giving your girl compliments. "When it comes to compliments, women are ravenous, bloodsucking monsters, always wanting more... more!" Homer Simpson said. And you'll receive a lot back if you give it to them." Yes, that is a bit excessive, but you may tell her how lovely she is, how much you enjoy her laugh, how lovely her eyes are, how intelligent she is, etc.

Try casually caressing as well. As you cross the street, extend your arm. Aid her in putting on her coat. Eliminate a flyaway hair from her face. You could even ask her to slow dance if the chance arises, but you should handle her carefully. Avoid grabbing or prodding her, and don't even try to touch any "high-risk" areas of her body.

Try a little flirting. Maintain eye contact.

You have a better chance of getting the woman to agree to a kiss if you are on a date. She must be attracted to you since she accepted your invitation. But the moment is probably unsuitable if she doesn't meet your gaze, pull away from your touch, or ignore your compliments.

Furthermore, it's always acceptable to beg to kiss her if you're truly uncomfortable. It is as easy as saying, "You know, I really like you and want to kiss you." Act like a man and tell her that she isn't ready. Just remark, "Sorry, I didn't mean to rush you," casually.

Remember that not everything that is rejected indicates failure. The first time my husband attempted to kiss me, I turned him down. Although I was drawn to him, I still wanted to learn more about him. Luckily, he's a fine guy; he graciously declined my invitation and made another one. It has been 12 years since we started dating.

Four: The Lead-Up to a Kiss

A man's lips can be sensual and charming when "teasing" a woman. A soft kiss on the hand or forehead is a romantic gesture that will probably leave her wanting more.

To give someone a hand kiss:

Cradle her fingers in yours and bring her hand to your lips. Maintain your focus on hers. That's not only hot but also allows you to gauge whether she's attracted to you or feels a little uneasy around you.

Bring her fingers up to meet your lips now. Never give her hand a back kiss. It's incredibly European and positively lovely to kiss her fingertips.

Your lips should only just barely touch the skin during the gentle kiss. After giving her a brief kiss, gently place her hand down.

Should you kiss her on the cheek or forehead? I wouldn't suggest kissing on the forehead unless you are somewhat taller than the girl. It's not attractive to drag her head down to your lips. Furthermore, it is improper to slump over a seated woman, despite what you may believe. That might sound a little frightening. Therefore, if your heights are similar, you could kiss each other on the cheek instead.

Once more, exercise extreme caution. You may lay one hand behind her neck and the other on her shoulders. Just slightly approach her, maintaining space between your bodies. Avoid appearing menacing. Give her a quick kiss on the forehead (or cheek), hold it briefly, and then move away.

Section Four

EVERYTHING CHANGES WITH SEX

Everything in a relationship is altered by sex. For most women, in particular, this is accurate. We rush into sex without thinking about the consequences, even though we all know this is accurate. Your brain's orbital frontal cortex, which is in charge of reason and self-control, is turned off during an orgasm. Right around the time your logical mind gives up, your body is overflowing with oxytocin, and you begin to connect with your lover. The stronger the glue, the more orgasmic you are. The problem is that women become extremely addicted to oxytocin. Our brains produce a "high" that we identify with the man we see. You want to be with him more and more the more strong the highs are.

An unreasonable bond to a man that permeates your logical thinking outside of the bedroom might be created via sex. Before you had sex, some traits would generally be deal breakers, but now they don't seem that horrible. You suffer from asthma, and he smokes cigars? You think, "It's nothing; I'll just carry an inhaler." After a few weeks, does your partner's lack of texts or other correspondence abruptly drop to almost nothing? No issue, you rationalize his actions because your rational mind is elsewhere. You can almost predict how having sex with someone will alter your expectations in a relationship if you know yourself fairly well.

Sharing our bodies with someone else can cause some people to go through a mental trance in which they start to hope that sex is more than just a physical act. Of course, times are changing, and a lot of people seem content with the notion that it was "just sex." After a certain number of those experiences, don't you start to yearn for something more gratifying on all levels? Are you sincerely content with one-night stands and casual sex? If you are, perhaps this book is not your thing.

Many people possess the ability to emit a sexual energy that draws others in. You may feel unique and convinced of their sincerity due to this energy. However, they may be acting out of ego rather than a genuine desire for deep connection and true intimacy, which require more than a few encounters to build. You may take sex to a much higher and more fulfilling level if you're willing to take a different route and limit your sexual activity to those with whom you truly connect on an emotional level and who appreciate the trip as much as the destination.

Why not hold off until you have mutual trust and a relationship commitment? Why give up on your body or soul? It is best to develop genuine, satisfying, and long-lasting connections gradually. Although having chemistry with someone is an incredible sensation, it does not necessarily mean that they are someone you should date or something more. It's common for sexual attraction to intensify with getting to know someone.

Think back to all the occasions when you may have hurried into a sexual encounter, and either the relationship ended abruptly, or you never heard from the other person. Many people can go on after having sex without experiencing inner turmoil. But you might not be that kind of person, and you can start to doubt your value because of someone else's rigidity, lack of confidence, emotional inaccessibility, or schedule.

Averaging six new sex encounters a year might build up to some really big figures, regardless of your age. You would have dated thirty people in just five years, and theoretically, you would have dated every person they had dated. There is a tenfold rise in the chances of STDs. You may easily run into multiple of your past partners in one night if you live in a relatively small city and frequent the major nightclubs! This can permanently damage your confidence and image, particularly if these incidents become part of your narrative. Consider yourself as you would a "brand," such as Ikea or Apple, if that helps. What comes to mind for someone when they hear your name brought up in a conversation? How are you seen in the dating and love industry, and what is your reputation? Setting boundaries is crucial if you want your brand to be unique and not the product of arbitrary societal standards that change dramatically over time.

Chapter 2: Etta R As soon as I began singing the final song of my performance, I met the most attractive, cheerful face I had ever imagined sitting at a table directly in front of the stage.

Even after all this time, Lee Lybrink could still weaken my knees with a single smile. It was unbelievable that we had already been together for five years. As I sang A Sunday Kind of Love directly at him, butterflies sprung in my stomach at the sight of him sitting there.

"I'm grateful." I gave a wave to the cheering patrons. "I'll return after a brief respite."

I securely held the stair railing while holding my long evening dress in one hand, and my imitation designer purse slung over my shoulder. Swan diving in front of a packed bar was the last thing I wanted to do, but falling down those steps in my heels was easy.

Had the experience. Completed that.

"To what am I due for this delightful surprise?" As I bent to kiss Lee's freshly shaven cheek, I inquired.

"Is it impossible for a man to leave work early to watch his girlfriend perform?" He extended his hand. "I have some news; sit down."

"Oh really?" I ordered a neat glass of brandy and sat down across from him.

Lee's expensive outfit made him seem lickable.

He said, "I received an offer from the company today for a new position."

I started to get excited and sat up taller. "Baby, that is incredible. Many congratulations.

We lifted our glasses in celebration of his recent achievement.

"I'm grateful. As he straightened the lapels, Lee fell silent. He took a deep breath, and his face contorted slightly. "But it's in San Francisco." He thumbed at the napkin beneath his seven and seven; he was usually jittery when anxious.

"When must you depart?" My heart began to sag. Due to his work, we relocated from Denver to New York. After months of detesting the busy city, I had just begun to adjust. Once more, we were being carried off.

"I'm heading out on the red eye in a few hours." He fixed his gaze on the table.

"I can meet you there next week after I pack up the apartment this weekend." With all the performances I would have to cancel and the arrangements I needed to make, my mind began to race.

Lee is well worth the effort. I kept reminding myself over and over. I was aware from the beginning of our relationship that I would have to give up things for his work even though I loved him without conditions. But how much longer would I have to create them? I had already left the University of Colorado, taken odd jobs throughout the years, and put my hopes of becoming a well-known singer on hold—forever.

"That's not it, Etta. He murmured, "You're not coming with me," and downed the remainder of his cocktail.

"Pardon me? What does that even imply in hell? He could not possibly be torturing me in this manner.

Lee clarified, saying, "My assistant already has my replacement taking over the flat. It's not our apartment; it belongs to the firm." Everything you own will be shipped back to your mother's house. I need your keys to get your overnight bag here. This Monday is the day that the new renters will move in. This will make or break my career, so I must give it my full attention. I can't worry about a romantic connection at this time.

"After everything we have gone through together, I can't believe you will end our relationship. Wait, don't even consider ending our relationship, and on top of all this nonsense, dump me on the streets of a city I never wanted to live in. I flung my hands up in the air, fighting back the sobs that threatened to burst my eyes.

You're twenty-two years old, see. I will be thirty years old soon. I can't spend my entire life with a youngster who sings in joke bars. We were in college, young, and enjoying ourselves.

This never ought to have progressed as far as it did. I felt the sharp edge of his cruel tone stabbing me.

As I stumbled to my feet, the words "I'm a joke?" flew out of my mouth.

Lee tried to encourage me to sit down again, reaching out a hand. "Please, Etta. Avoid creating a commotion. You had to have anticipated this.

Not at all. I cherish you. But it seems like I'm simply trash that you may discard. An old, filthy rag that you've stopped using and have just thrown away. I grabbed my keyring and took off the gold key to my old house, placing it on the table before him.

This is what's going to work out best for us both. You can now, at last, pursue your aspirations. He seemed so relieved, and I despised it. I detested everything that was taking place.

I grabbed the water glass in front of him and hurled its contents in his direction. "Go fuck yourself, please. Enjoy your life, dickface.

He got up quickly and started shouting after me as I hurried to the woman's room. "Etta! You always do things like this. "Queen of drama!"

A fucking asshat, that one.

I leaned up against the small bathroom door and locked it.

Simply inhale.

I would have to return to that blasted stage in ten minutes, and I was going crazy.

Lee Lybrink was the ultimate, in my opinion. How stupid could I have been?

In my entire life, I had never felt so innocent.

I gripped the porcelain sink and tried to think of what my mother would say if she were here as I looked at myself in the mirror.

"ETTA?" Through the crack in my bedroom door, my mother called.

"Please leave," I cried into my pillow.

She slipped into my bed's foot as soon as she entered. "You know I can't do that, honey," I said. Speak with me.

"There's nothing to discuss." I moved away from her even more.

"What's upsetting you so much, Etta?"

"Not a thing!" I sulked and threw a throw pillow at her from over my shoulder.

She laughed and touched my leg. "I truly won't be leaving anytime soon. Leak.

I sat up and sighed, "Okay. In front of the entire school, Julius ended our relationship in the cafeteria today.

My mother forced an understanding smile on her face, clearly relieved. "Someone doesn't belong in your life if you beg them to be."

"My life has come to an end. I will never be allowed to walk into that school again. You must homeschool me.

"Etta, don't be too emotional. For crying out loud, you are just fourteen. Men will pass through your life. Just remember that a lousy chapter does not indicate the end of the story.

"Why can't you just act like a typical mother and call him out for what he did? The prefabricated proverbial quotes irritate me.

Alright. He is a rude person. He's a fucking useless piece of donkey dung. She gave me a close-lipped smile, and then we both started laughing.

www.ingramcontent.com/pod-product-compliance
Lightning Source LLC
Chambersburg PA
CBHW052135110526
44591CB00012B/1736